CHAPTER & VERSE

POEMS OF JEWISH IDENTITY

CHAPTER & VERSE

POEMS OF JEWISH IDENTITY

DAN BELLM

ROSE BLACK

CHANA BLOCH

RAFAELLA DEL BOURGO

MARGARET KAUFMAN

JACQUELINE KUDLER

MELANIE MAIER

MURRAY SILVERSTEIN

SUSAN TERRIS

SIM WARKOV

CONFLUX PRESS, PRESCOTT, ARIZONA

ISBN: 978-0-9826024-3-0

Cover image: Stained-glass window (detail) from Congregation Emanu-El, San Francisco, California. At Emanu-El, the Great Windows—designed by San Francisco artist Mark Adams and installed in 1972 and 1973—face each other in the main sanctuary. Water (east), shown here, and Fire (west) symbolize the two mystical elements of creation.

Cover photograph by Ethan Kaplan, www.kaplanphotography.com

Yehuda Amichai quote from "On the Day I Left", translated from the Hebrew by Chana Bloch, is from the *Selected Poetry of Yehuda Amichai*, edited and translated by Chana Bloch and Stephen Mitchell. (c) 1996 by Chana Bloch and Stephen Mitchell. Published by the University of California Press and reprinted with permission from the University of California Press.

Cover & book design by Tania Baban-Natal, Conflux Press, www.confluxpress.com

Printed in the United States of America.

I travel light, like the prayers of Jews.
I lift off simply as a glance, or a flight
to some other place.

—Yehuda Amichai

CONTENTS

INTRODUCTION

Not only is the act of writing for history difficult, it is heroic, as any pitting of the living will against the dark must be, and as a result it redefines heroic as something *ordinary.*

A record of the ordinary, at its best, will be unflinching, as it is in this anthology of poems of Jewish identity by ten Bay Area poets. While these poems evoke the beautiful loam and moonlight of an old world and culture, they also are blunt in reporting the terrible. *Chapter & Verse* is filled with people from the old country who had ineluctable destinies. Nonetheless, the scent of hay, apples, cloves, pomade, shoe polish, and steaming potatoes permeates their narratives.

Reconciling with her own Jewish identity, the poet Adrienne Rich described her process in her 1982 essay "Split at the Root":

> It comes to me that in order to write this, I have to be willing to do two things; I have to claim my father, for I have my Jewishness from him and my gentile mother, and I have to break his silence, his taboos; in order to claim him, I have in a sense to expose him.
>   And there is, of course, the third thing: I have to face the sources and the flickering presence of my own ambivalences as a Jew...

One has only to think of other poetic giants such as Celan and Amichai, and of the incandescence and moral intelligence of their language, to come to terms with the responsibilities that pertain for poets of Jewish identity. It takes fierce desire and dedication to excavate memories and enter into a dialogue with history. The struggle is essentially a struggle against death. This present anthology takes reconstitution as its challenge and commitment. While reading it, I am reminded of another anthology, *Against Forgetting*, for which editor Carolyn Forché selected poems "to understand the impress of extremity upon the poetic imagination." The poems of *Chapter & Verse* reveal deep pressures and fissures of the Jewish experience.

We owe these poets a debt for nurturing the world of rich Jewish culture for those of us distanced from, or unfamiliar with, its sensorial territory. We are suspended a while in the atmosphere of ripe figs and pickled herring, where horseradish grows "tall along the fence." This territory is also abundant with philosophical inquiry, as sustaining and essential as milk and honey.

Jane Miller
Oakland, California
June 2010

FLOUR AND ASH

"Make flour into dough," she answers,
 "and fire will turn it into food.
Ash is the final abstraction of matter.
You can just brush it away."

She tacks a sheet of paper to the wall,
dips her hand in a palette of flour and ash,
applies the fine soft powders with a fingertip,
highlighting in chalk and graphite,
blending, blurring with her thumb.
Today she is working in seven shades of gray.

Outside the door, day lilies
in the high flush of summer-
about-to-be-fall. Her garden burns
red and yellow in the dry August air
and is not consumed.

Inside, on the studio wall, a heavy
particulate smoke
thickens and rises. Footsteps grime the snow.
The about-to-be-dead line up on the ramp
with their boxy suitcases,
ashen shoes.

When I get too close she yanks me back.
She hovers over her creation
though she too has a mind
to brush against that world
and wipe it out.

POTATO EATERS

My grandmother never did learn to write.
"Making love" was not in her lexicon;
I wonder if she ever took off her clothes
when her husband performed his conjugal duties.
She said God was watching,
reciting Psalms was dependable medicine,
a woman in pants an abomination.

In their hut on the Dniester
six children scraped the daily potatoes from a single plate;
each one held a bare spoon.

Five years from the shtetl her daughters
disguise themselves
in lisle stockings and flapper dresses.
The boys slick their hair with pomade.
What do they remember of Russia? "Mud."

That's grandma in the center. At ease in owl glasses.
"Don't run, you'll fall."
Mostly she keeps her mouth shut; the children
would rather not hear.
What does a full stomach know
of an empty stomach?

It's time you opened your mouth, *bobbe*;
I'm old enough now to ask you a thing or two
and you're too dead to be annoyed.
You'll know where to find me,
I'm the daughter of your second son.
I have the spoons.

THE NEW WORLD

My uncle killed a man and was proud of it.
Some punk with a knife came at him in Flatbush
and he knocked the sucker to the ground.
The sidewalk finished the job.

By then he'd survived two wives
and a triple bypass. He carried
a bit of the plastic tubing in his pocket
and would show it to anyone.
He'd unbutton his shirt right there on the street
and show off the scar.

As a boy, he watched a drunken Cossack
go after his father with an ax.
His sister tried to staunch the bleeding
with a hunk of dry bread.

That's the old country for you:
they ate with their hands, went hungry to bed,
slept in their stink. When pain knocked,
they opened the door.

The bitter drive to Brooklyn every Sunday
when I was a child—
Uncle George in the doorway snorting and laughing,
I'm gonna take a bite of your little behind.

He was a good-looker in a pin-striped suit
and shoeshine shoes.
_This is America, we don't live
in the Dark Ages anymore, sweetie.
This is a free country._

BROTHERS

When I was the Baba Yaga of the house
on my terrible chicken legs,
the children sat close on the sofa as I read,
both of them together
determined to be scared.

Careful! I cackled, stalking them
among the pillows:
You bad Russian boy,
I eat you up!
They shivered and squirmed, my delicious sons,

waiting for a mighty arm
to seize them.
I chased them screeching down the hall,
I catch you, I eat you!
my witch-blade hungry for the spurt
of laughter—

        What stopped me
even as I lifted my hand?
The stricken voice that cried: *Eat him!*
Eat my brother.

THE MESSIAH OF HARVARD SQUARE

Every year some student would claim to be the Messiah.
It was the rabbi who had to deal with them.
He had jumped, years ago, from a moving boxcar
on the way to a death camp. That leap
left him ready for anything.

This year at Pesach, a Jewish student proclaimed
Armageddon. "Burn the books! Burn the textbooks!"
he shouted to a cheerful crowd,
sang Hebrew songs to confuse the Gentiles,
dressed for the end like Belshazzar.
People stopped to whisper and laugh.

"I have a noble task," the boy explained.
"I must prepare myself to endure
the laughter of fools."

The rabbi was a skeptic.
Years ago he'd been taught, If you're planting a tree
and someone cries out, *The Messiah has come!*
finish planting the tree. Then
go see if it's true.

Still, he took the boy into his study
and questioned him slowly, meticulously,
as if the poor soul before him might be,
God help us, the Messiah.

THE DARK OF DAY

We were trying to keep things neat and shiny.
Twenty-four years.
We had two sets of dishes—one for love,
one for hate. We kept them in separate cupboards.
Eat love and hate at the same meal
and you'll get punished.

The rabbis taught us the mathematics of dividing
this from that. They certified
the micro-moment when day tips over
into night: *When the third star presents itself in the sky.*
They drew a line through that eye of light, a longitude.
You've got to navigate the evening blessing
with precision, not one star too soon.
But night comes on slowly.
It takes all day.

My friend's father was killed
in a car crash. She hated him,
hadn't seen him in years.
When the police called, she drove to the ditch
where his wrecked Chevy waited for the tow truck.

The body was gone. On the dashboard, broken glasses,
an open notebook splotched with his blood.
Then she was crying, not knowing why.
She tore out a stain on the mottled paper,
his ragged last breath,
and took it into her mouth.

THE CONVERTS

On the holiest day we fast till sundown.
I watch the sun stand still
as the horizon edges towards it. Four hours to go.
The rabbi's mouth opens and closes and opens.
I think: fish
and little steaming potatoes,
parsley clinging to them like an ancient script.

Only the converts, six of them in the corner,
in their prayer shawls and feathery beards,
sing every syllable.
What word
are they savoring now?
If they go on loving that way, we'll be here all night.

Why did they follow us here, did they think
we were happier?
Did someone tell them we knew
the lost words
to open God's mouth?

The converts sway in white silk,
their necks bent forward in yearning
like swans,
and I covet
what they think we've got.

THE ALPHABET

*[H]ebrew vowel pointings hang like motes, as if they were
the molecules the consonants breathed.*
    —Edmund Wilson

Ten years old and I recite the *Hear O Israel*
again and again. I mouth God's promise
to Abram to form a people whose numbers
would multiply and exceed the stars
in the Babylonian skies of Southern Iraq.

And I learn there's more than one way
to look at the world. Roman letters run left to right
during public school hours of 9 to 4;
Hebrew letters, right to left, from 4:45
to 6:30 at the Talmud Torah—

and my literary avatar, Edmund Wilson,
starts on the same right stuff at age fifty eight
I run across the word *mote* and the first thing
that comes to mind is Book-of-Matthew's
beam in your brother's eye, or your own.

Then I find the engineers latch on to *mote*
to describe something they call *smart dust*,
yes, *smart dust*; a computing circuit
the size of a grain of sand or even smaller.
Assemble them into a deck of playing cards

and it's a computer center. As for the beam of light
shining on the Hebrew marks that encircle
the consonants: they're like a pack of Comanches
besieging the wagon train in a 1930's movie
John Ford makes out in Monument Valley.

Those dots and dashes are placed
above the consonant, below the consonant,
following the consonant. Consonant
after consonant trudges across the Hebrew page
right to left on a golden Manitoba afternoon

while other boys chase a soccer ball.

CLEFT HOOF

*Whatsoever parteth the hoof and is wholly cloven-footed
and cheweth the cud, that may ye eat.*
Lev.11:20–22.

Cleft hoof—the kind my ancestors would avoid
when the creature did not chew its cud;
the kind that ends up as mushu pork,
baked Virginia ham, Canadian bacon
and steamed clams.

Culinary handcuffs are good enough
for those who believe, believe;
but I found relief from the ban
on milk mixed with meat,
the ban on unscaled fish and shellfish.

Like many of us I savored the table's savories;
seated myself next to the Roman sage Epicurus
and in an act of hubris, turned my back
on the Book of Leviticus.

THE GREEN FELT FIELDS

draw me to the grimy Nordic Pool Hall
peopled by roughnecks, ne'er-do-wells
and high school students.

There I plant the weight of my body
on the left leg, firmly; my right leg stretched
along the billiard table rim.

Thumb and forefinger of the left hand
bridge a cue stick to send a volley
ricocheting off the far end of the table:

a contest of wills
in the manly game of eight-ball.
My adversaries are keen to test their worth;

all of us, part-time pool-hall hangers-on
in hot pursuit of eight-ball—

especially Denny, who has read,
he says, all of Joyce's *Ulysses*
but not a word in Hebrew of the poet

Chaim Nachman Bialik.

MEZUZAH ON MY MIND

A small case affixed to the right doorpost. In the case,
a tiny scroll; parchment, handwritten in black ink.
The Creed copied by a scribe reads: _Hear O Israel_. . . .

I notice how the mezuzah is placed: not vertical
not horizontal but at an angle—on the bias.
A Rabbinic compromise.
They couldn't agree which way to go.

If I were devout, every time I'd pass through a door
with a mezuzah on it I'd touch it then kiss the fingers
that touched it; that way remind myself constantly
of the _613 mitzvoth_ that the believer should embrace.

I was summoned to observe some of them:
meat versus milk, blessings, Shabbat
and prayers, High Holidays and the lesser days.

As a child, I did, but not for long.
James Joyce had his Jesuit teachers.
I had my _melam'dim_.
I too lost the faith but still carry the baggage.

My apartment's doorpost is mezuzah-free
but even now, if asked I could recite
Hear O Israel.

I'm in exile with the Golden Calf of California.
Like the backsliding Hebrew slaves in the desert
yearning for the lure of Egypt I relish

. . . the onions, and the cucumbers,
and the melons,
_and the leeks, and the garlic. . . ._*

We are all in exile from the moment
we're born; each of us, the slackers
and the pious steered by our own mezuzah,
be it horizontal, vertical or on the bias.

* Numbers 5:11

21

TETRAGRAMMATON

Right Hand Man Speaks

It's okay to say: Lord, Master, the Unknowable, the Ineffable,
the All Merciful. You may say: *adonai   elohim*
but you don't say His Name based on four Hebrew letters

yod he vav he.

The Greeks call Him *Tetragrammaton.*

We can all agree on that. Just don't say *His Hebrew Name.*
You can count on Him—or you can't. If you are swallowed
by a whale, you can. If Zyklon B gas fills
the shower chamber, you can't. You don't carve Him
in stone. You don't paint Him in oil; you don't see Him
in the flesh. He's the Biblical One. Never Two.
Never Three. *That's Trinity.* You don't cross Him.
You don't cross yourself. When you're done
you don't cross River Styx.

Blasphemy

At the foot of the mountain I curl on the studio floor
in ritual dance; fear to call out the forbidden name
of the Hebrew God, the One beyond touch,
beyond utterance. *Never mind! Let go!*
Over waves of sound I bellow: *Yahweh! Yahweh!*
It's anathema to utter His Name, a *shandeh,*
but I don't stop. *Yahweh! Yahweh!*
I succumb to the pagans: we shout, shake, scatter;
consort with spirits Abraham thought he put away
when he smashed the idols in his father's house,
packed his camels' bags, carried off his two wives,
got the hell out of *Ur Kasdim*
and lit out for Canaan.
Yahweh! Yahweh!

I turn inward, burning with the four Hebrew letters
my forefathers would never have forsaken,
would never have spurned.

SABBATH AT STARBUCKS IN LOS GATOS

. . . and lanky fillies in low-slung jeans
swish by my table
Asian tattoos two inches above the cleft
abs taut as all hell—
and I rally to their full-frontal views
and I'm in awe of these fragrant pagans
flaunting their youth arm's length
from small-town Daddy Mommy
Father Joe and Sister Teresa
and I jazz the secular English
at the very hour my grandfather
the *Zaydeh* would be studying
a page of Talmud in Hebraic Aramaic
at a shul near Burrows Avenue
when I was a kid in corduroy britches.

NEWS FROM ANDALUSIA

If you ask the dead they'll rip the lid
off your tendencies, your singular sin.
Should you deny it, your mouth and body language
shall say you do—because you lie.
—Samuel the Prince (c. 1000)

Now, a millennium later
The Prince of Granada still asks about *your* singular sin

And mine

Even though I have committed more than one
Such as violation of the Sabbath

Insolent disrespect for Yahweh's Name
And others I won't tally

To be sure, I have never killed
Nor have I borne false witness against my neighbor

In baseball talk, a two-hundred hitter
A minor-league moral figure

Overloaded by strikeouts
Foul balls fly balls bungled bunts

And you:
What's your batting average?

LOT'S WIFE
     (after Akhmatova)

They had no time—the just man
hurried across the bridge,
followed God's magistrate
along the black ridge.

His grieving wife lagged behind
as if she had no will,
arms heavy with useless things,
heart heavier still.

She couldn't recall if she'd shut the door,
turned off the iron; worse guilt,
she'd left behind the baby pictures,
her mother's ring, her wedding quilt.

One arm raised as if to gather
her whole life in that embrace,
tears blurring the view,
without much thought she turned her face,

became what she had shed. Who grieves
for this nameless woman, Lot's reflective wife?
I grieve.
I know holding on can cost a life.

PAINT

Last week there were windows on that wall.
Sheetrocked, taped, sanded clean.
The bookcases pulled away,
skeleton designs.
When can you stop thinking of those graves?

Anne Frank, those hidden attic rooms,
and on the television only last week,
a man from New Jersey took his grown sons
to the Ukraine, showed them the root cellar
where his neighbor (still alive) risked his life
to hide his Jewish friends.

I sit in the middle of packed-up belongings
and cry. Something about luck mixed with
shame at how easy this life is.
Everything is proceeding smoothly,
the house painter rolls "Bauhaus Buff"

over the long walls, obliterating
the dark-smudged dog graffiti
our black dog, now dead, rubbed in
with years of back-scratching.
That dog loved me unconditionally.

Surely now is the time for looking forward.
Stop thinking of the dog, the millions,
the ineradicable losses.

WHEN THE RADIO

Sometimes when I can't remember
several minutes go by
                when I'm in a room
or when the radio

Several minutes go by
when I'm cleaning out the icebox
                or when the radio
music is music I *know* but can't name

Sometimes when I'm cleaning out the icebox
lifting plastic sacks of spoiled zucchini
                                music I *know* but can't name
I find food never opened,   its shelf life outlived

Lifting sacks of spoiled zucchini
the memorial service from Grace Cathedral is broadcast,
                food that's outlived its shelf life,   never opened
I *know* but cannot sing the words

The memorial service from Grace Cathedral is broadcast
It's September 12, the day after,   *Erev Rosh Hashanah*
                I know the music but cannot sing those words,
try,   but my voice falters

September 12, the day after,   *Erev Rosh Hashanah*
Sometimes when I'm in a room,
                try,   but my voice falters
several minutes go by   can't remember   when the radio

TAWNY AVATAR

Somewhere my father is dying,
but I am in a room with the lemon light
of beachfront property. Drying moss
cushions one wall, pads the planks

of an upstairs bedroom where my aunt and I
puzzle over the odd footprint in the moss.
Tall windows in this room of filtered light
glean the hills and bluff behind the house

for signs of life beyond the beachfront walk;
my father is dying somewhere.
The footprint seems a cougar's, but how stalk
into a room so wild a thing, how dare

encroach upon this house, and where,
having stolen into this room,
is he, huge shadow, tawny avatar,
sliding along a wall, forecasting doom?

My aunt is sure he has left the place:
we both recall that strange baby-crying
mewl we woke to in fog of morning's grace.
Back home my father is dying

but I can't get to him, leave the house,
not while the cougar might be hiding
down the hall or behind a mossy couch.
He's left his mark—he may be biding

his own sweet time, crouched downstairs,
tawny avatar, shadow of death enraged
and merciless between me and where
somewhere, uncaged, my father is dying.

OCTOBER

Ripe figs dot the lawn
between October wind and jays.
Let birds feast—you're gone,
and I've no appetite these days.

TWO YEARS LATER, YARHZEIT

I.

The squat white candle sits
on the sideboard, shrouded in dust.
Day after day the calendar submits
to one damned thing after another, *just*

how it is, the way it goes,
How quickly it passes, Look!
Has it been a whole year since—? No,
then *Yes.* The match is struck.

II.

But that isn't what I meant to write at all, tidy, short-rhymed lines.
I want a Ginsberg wail, want to evoke the weird reverence
that *yarhzeit* seems to kindle,
setting out for the market to buy the candle
where it's always found among the kosher foods.
I can keen at Mollie Stone's as well as Ginsberg,
borscht, horseradish, red-eyed, so candle,
kindle me home and lit, last twenty-four hours: *mark it.*
I remember so much, their voices, her short cough, how
they sustain me in this life: tangle of her "Careful, now—"
his "You can do anything you want."

I remember *them,* but then recall our evening plans.
Uh, oh: that dance between respect and safety
ending in a twirl of cautious severance,
candle moved into the kitchen sink
where it can't catch anything else on fire.

THE STARTING HOUR

Lichen clings on oak outside my window. Light
shapes the silver, the shadowed branch tawny
as deer haunch in the ivy beneath the tree,
time marked by birdcall, vinca blooming or not,
the scene finite and specific as a Book of Hours.

Our downslope neighbor appeared at the door
to warn of oak blight and chain saws,
seven oaks lost on his place. It was as if
the clock needed resetting. Our trees look fine:
for how long? *This tree, this oak.*

Those davening know it's time to pray when they can
separate the dark threads of their prayer shawls
from the light. When I can, from my pillow,
distinguish one leaf from another, time to move
into each day the way squirrels move,

first with caution, then with a leaping joy.
They sometimes rest, paws up, as if in prayer.
Today, also, deep sorrow: memorial service,
light to dark too soon.
I pray in spite of dubious belief.

Prayers rise unsteadily, belief one wing,
unbelief the other. Falter altogether
when the neighbors gut their house,
expand into the place where live oaks died.
Our ravine rattles each morning at the legal

starting hour. Buzz saw and hammer
separate dawn from day, rattle the peace
with each distinctive sound.
My darling holds me until his shoulder aches,
the squirrel's sequence: caution to joy to prayer.

INSIDE

they are sitting in the living room weeping, all of them shaking tears. I run from one to the other, touching hands, their knees. Don't cry, don't cry, I say. They don't look at me. They keep on crying. The room gets dark and no one turns on the lights.

Mother and Grandpa Abe are there, and all the aunts are there. Faye, Esther, Hilda, Norma and Rhoda. The uncles, Victor and David. Lace doilies on the backs and arms of chairs.

Where is Grandma Sarah?

Something that has no business here has come into the room. Something that belongs far away from us, beyond the dining room, with table made from the box piano taken apart. Something that belongs beyond the yard, picnic table, grape arbor, horseradish tall along the fence.

Beyond the factory across the street where Grandpa presses pants, corner saloon buckets of beer. Beyond the Slotnicks, the Villasanas, the Frankels, the Einenkels and the Morris Street Shul. Beyond the empty lot with old quince trees, butterflies, wild berries.

Something that belongs far away has come inside.

BAD SHEEP

They didn't talk about the past, but the word *Catholic* made Dad make a tight white fist and pound the table, shout *Irresponsible Breeding!* or *Holy Water! Why don't they pour it into oceans, purify the world?* The word *Catholic* made the pale pink dishes shake and fresh green beans and squash just sit there, cold. I knew that *Catholic* was buried in a secret trunk upstairs—Henry, First Communion, 1909.

Jewish was my mother's word. It made her wring her hands and cry, sniffle down at me, say, *I'll never be accepted in a synagogue again!* It made her grab my arm and say, *You don't know anything ABOUT Jewish, do you? You don't know anything at all.*

Catholic came in pamphlets through the mail. A shepherd was searching for sheep who had strayed from the fold. Bad sheep. Confused and lonely sheep. A shepherd's crook was going to pull them back. Dad said, *Goddamn Catholics, Goddamn them.*

Jewish and *Catholic* were told to leave our house. But they didn't pay any attention. They burst through all the doors and windows. They swarmed around our heads. *Jewish* covered up the mirrors. *Catholic* confessed in a black booth, said *Hail-Mary-Full-of-Grace. Jewish* had a ram's horn. A room with men and women divided.

Between these words a bridge of secret languages, lit candles, long robes. Sweet wine. I stand in the middle, toss *Jewish/Catholic* over the edge. Over and over. Then fish them up again. Slippery, hard to hold.

Catholic made Dad drink a teaspoon full of holy water every night before he went to bed. *Jewish* said, *You can't read the piece about A Virtuous Woman at Aunt Esther's funeral, because it is a Jewish prayer and after all, you are only half. Jewish* said, *Don't worry, by Jewish law you'll always be Jewish, don't worry.*

ABRAM'S MOUNTAIN

Four doors lead to the inside of a mountain. She does not know which to choose, but decides to crawl through the smallest, into a damp and cold passage, where she needs to bend and twist in order to fit. Perhaps she'll be safe there. She slowly makes her way towards the mountain's center. She dreams of an eagle's nest, high on a cliff overlooking the sea. She dreams of blue sky and giants who live in the clouds. She dreams of the greenest fields, and rich black ones being plowed by four milk-white horses. The fields are planted with barley and rye, which Great-Grandfather Abram grinds in his mill at the Shtetl of Kölno. The walls of the mill are moonstone. It stands beside a stream with a mighty current. The stones in the streambed are emeralds and rubies. At night Great-Grandfather Abram swims naked with lustrous fishes, and when Cossacks come to murder him, after the Cossacks ride through and murder the men and the women and children, all that is left are the cakes made from barley and rye. The Cossacks devour these too. They eat so much that they grow into mountains, mountains covered with barley and rye that sway in the wind.

A HISTORY OF POLAND

On the maps I colored in at school I made it pink. I never thought of it as having grass or trees, blue rivers, lakes. Germany and Russia were on two sides, and the Russian side had dots from where Poland used to be before a bunch of it got moved over into Russia. When I was older I learned about pogroms, where Jews were rounded up and killed. The killers came on horseback. Then the Nazis came through, and the Russians came through from the other side. Lots of Jews used to live in Poland.

My great-uncle Joe, who is one hundred years old, lived in Poland until he was six. He lived in a shtetl called Kölno, near the city Lomza. Then he came to America on a boat, with his parents, Rifka and Abraham, and his sisters, Ida and Sarah, my grandmother.

They're all dead now, except Uncle Joe, and I need to ask him about Poland. When I talk with him, sometimes he's there and sometimes not.

> We had a mill! Uncle Joe shouts. *A windmill or a water mill?* A windmill! We made flour! We baked all kinds of things! *What kind of flour?* How should I know, all kinds of flour! *Maybe barley, wheat, rye.* The Polish people worked for us! Gentiles! We had fifty gentiles working for us! We had to speak Polish to them! There was Yiddish at home, but we had to speak Polish to the gentiles! I want to know, did you go to Temple on Yom Kippur?

> *No, Uncle Joe, but soon I'm going to light the Yahrzeit candle for my mother.*

> Good, good, that's good, light the Yahrzeit for your mother. You must remember. My father took me to synagogue in Lomza! He took me to the Great Synagogue there! It was destroyed in the war. Now it's gone.

> *But the windmill, Uncle Joe, maybe the windmill's still in Poland.*

The windmill is big. A field of wheat surrounds it. It is made of wood. It has a millstone, and it faces into the wind. It smells like cake.

TORAH IN THE BASEMENT

I steal it from the synagogue, while others chant
in Hebrew on both sides of the aisle. I do not have a part

and must find one. I clutch the Torah to my chest and run.
The rabbi running behind me booms, *You have no right!*

His white beard shakes as he tries to pry the Torah
from my hands. *Look*, I cry, *Great-Grandfather Abram*

*owned a mill in the Shtetl of Kölno! He prayed in the Great
Synagogue of Lomza! He fought off Cossacks!*

Not. Good. Enough. Still running, I find the basement
stairs, wind down to the bottom, to the spiders,

coal dust, cracked cement, old and broken things.
In my arms the Torah scroll rocks back and forth.

Don't drop it. I want to lay it down beside the yellow
names and dates. Hard to leave behind. Hard to carry.

WASHING THE BODY

I walk the rocky cliffs above the Potomac
early November the maples blaze orange
and red, and when I return my brother hugs
me hard and fast and that's how I am told.
We walk into our mother's bedroom, check
for breath and pulse. And no one tells us

what we might do next, sit with her, wash
her slowly. We haven't asked. Our mother's
Jewish past would have instructed us, had
we wanted to know. Our Great-Uncle Joe
could have told us that our mother would
linger awhile, near her body, confused.

*From the moment of death the body is not left
alone until burial.* That she must be tended
and washed. A pure act, because the dead
cannot give back. But we brother and sister
half-Jews, Jews among non-Jews, non-Jews
among Jews, we have it figured out. We call

a man to take away the body. Take it away
fast as he can, reduce it to ash and fragments
of bone. Typical weight for adult female,
four pounds. Is this what Mother wanted?
We scatter her from a bridge above Great
Falls, and who knows how far she will travel

in the cold fast river below. Where is she?
Mother, I want to wash you gently.
I want to wash you with warm water,
as children are washed when born.
I want to scent the water with myrtle
and wash you, from head to foot.

I want to pare your nails and comb
your hair, wrap your body in a white
linen shroud, put you in a simple pine
box. Lay you in earth. Each time I visit,
I will bring you a stone, and place it
on your grave. Stone of your name.

INVITATION

half of me from pickled herring in New York
half of me from fields of corn in Indiana

all my mother's ancestors from Poland
all my father's from Alsace-Lorraine

all the Jews who came before my mother
all the Catholics who came before my father

all who came before Jewish and Catholic
ever existed, before the pyramids of Egypt

and the great circles of upright stones
all who go back to beyond the fertile crescent

those who were not me who became me
tonight you are all invited

to gather around the fire
to share flat bread and ancient beans.

GLASS

You enter through a storefront,
window emblazoned:
MAX STRAUS, GLASS—

on this night, shades drawn
against the bladed eyes
of strangers. Inside, the seder
table runs lengthwise down

the room, balanced between
ceiling-high racks of glass
sheets shelved end to end,
green edges glistening. On

all other nights, he'd be
just now shuffling through
the door, settling his handcart
of mirrors and windows to

rest, but on this night,
already in place at the head
of his table, flanked by uncles,
he commences the mysterious

guttural drone, pausing only
to perform such miracles as
the text requires. All of
your life when you think of

him, you think of him like
this: blue crystal flicker of eyes
between high, wide cheekbones,
gnarled forefinger touching

once each: egg, bitter herbs,
shank bone, matzoh—*Behold
the bread of our affliction*—
dipping one at a time, from

out of his kiddush cup, ten
plagues, each a bead of red
wine on a milk-glass plate.

THE WORLD WAS JEWISH

"Make a _shimel lechol_ in the old man's back
And someone sticks his finger IN."

Eyes closed, you leaned cross-armed against
the big elm on Seventeenth Street, waited for
the poke in the back, then counted to twenty
so everyone had time to hide. "Hine-go-seek"
we called it, and as for the incantation to start
the game, its source was a mystery to us,
much as the world was mostly mystery then,
except the funny words we knew for sure were
Jewish, much as the world was Jewish—
at least from Ocean Avenue to Ocean Parkway
and four subway stops in any direction from
                              the city to the sea:

mezuzahs anchored head-high at every front-
door frame, fathers trudging down Sixteenth
each morning to the subway, sample cases
steady in hand; mothers sweet-talking the
kosher butcher on the corner of Fourteenth
("For you darling, I save a special cut."),
grandmas sitting outside the lobbies on
folding chairs, serene as teakettles,
all of it—the neighborhood—buttressed by
the Avenue R temple on one end, the Avenue
                              P shul on the other.

News of the world beyond Brooklyn arrived
via the big Philco radio in the living room—
Sunday nights listening to Eddie Cantor,
Jack Benny, and the music of Artie Shaw
who, it appeared, was Grandpa's third cousin
(the name was Arshawsky) and who, in a bold
burnishing of the family crest, had married
                              Lana Turner!

Lana Turner—that platinum-lit, satin-smiled
sweater girl, who had just vaulted past Hedy
Lamarr to claim first place on my Favorites list—
was married to Artie Shaw, which meant that
        Lana Turner was my fourth cousin!

Except that first cousin Marilyn, who was
from New Jersey and knew such things said
that Lana was a "shiksa," which meant, she
explained, that Lana Turner wasn't Jewish—

a small truth that stunned at first, then slipped
in slowly, the way a small pill slips in—one
with sustained-release action that alters
internal equilibriums over time—a general
shift in the body's tectonic balance. It wasn't
long before Lamarr regained her primary place
in my affections, which worked out better
anyway, seeing as how her hair was dark,
                    like mine.

SARAH

Each month, the terrible
blood, skull of a moon
gaping to a barren sky.
What could it matter to
me, the covenant they
cooked between them on
the sizzling plain of
Moreh—he and his God
negotiating the limits
of land, obligation, the
projected revenues of my
womb, while the Egyptian
whore lorded it over me,
her belly swelling before
my eyes—a great pustule
rising from the center of
my pain. What do I care
for Canaan or a Void that
does not choose to speak
to me? What would I want
with a nation, needing
only the kingdom of
a single baby's touch?

LOT'S WIFE

Hurry! he hissed through his teeth,
Hurry! all morning as I loaded
my life onto three handcarts. *Can't
you smell it,* he bawled, *the place
stinks of sinning! Sinning,* he said,
who only last night offered our
daughters up like just-picked figs
to two hollow-eyed strangers. Only
an animal doesn't look back. How
can I know where I'm going without
knowing where I've been? I turned
to see the sweet curve of the hill
above my home—my mother, arm
still raised, grown small—pale as
a moth in the glitter of the noon
sky. Then nothing.   Salt.   Of tears
sweat   semen.   Only an animal
has no name. My mother named me
Zachora.   It means Remember.

REVELATION

For every exile who walked out
of Egypt between walls of water,
for everyone who remembered
the feel of sea bottom underfoot,
the sibilant roar of water rearing
on the right, on the left, someone
forgot. Someone scanning

the dry horizon for a well,
or already mourning the musky
smell of autumn in her father's
fig trees, forgot the hosannahs,
and, by the bitter waters of Marah,
forgot the flash of dancing feet,
the shimmer of timbrels.

For every proselyte at Sinai,
someone never heard the horns
at all. Someone turned back from
the mountain to bank the fire,
feed the baby, steal a secret
moment with another.

Revelation begins in attention:
while the elders trembled before
the word of God flowing down
the scorched north flank of Sinai,
someone, rising from a last long
embrace, gazed into the rapt face
of the beloved and saw
that it was good.

SARA

Toward the end, she took to dozing
in the Torah class, seated as always
at the rabbi's right hand, hair swept
up in an elegant tumble of umber
and ash.
        Still, the old ferocity
smoldered there, never more than
an eyelash flicker away: *What
is the essence of faith?* the strict
Brooklyn bark biting off the edges of
each question, the old Bolshevik fervor
burning behind coke-bottle glasses.
"What is the meaning of my long life?"
less a question than a challenge,
less a challenge than a prayer.

And, at the very end, in failing light,
when all the answers hovered just
above her bed, bright wings braced
for takeoff, someone questioned if
it wasn't time to send for the rabbi?
No, she whispered. *Not now.*
I've no time for chit-chat now.

IN THE BEGINNING

And Grandson Leo comes to mind, squealing
With joy in my arms last week when I slobbered
With joy on his tummy, then, back flex'd—the colic!—
Something so quickly so wrong, struggling
To arch himself free, free of this the slobbering world.

If the body is in pain—and it is—before it learns
To talk, are vowels the remnants of howls,
Each word a vanished lullaby? To soothe
The ache of all that creating? The body _is_
At birth a wreck; sore and sorry: _what shore is this?_

Here's Leo, being changed, the promise
Of some eventual saying: churning at nothing,
Hands reaching out to clasp then miss then clasp again—
What's me? What's not? The thoughts, Leo, a body
Must tend! To which I add maker, the maker

Of shits. (And maker of shits-not-even, as when
Your little brow was ploughed with furrows
And, _Thought!_ I said to your pa, _Naa,_ said Jake, _gas._)
(I should have guessed. Digest, digest! I was a brain-
Riddled body once, sucked the breast _what's-me?_

Gnawed the bone _what's-not?_) (But doesn't
It long to be thought, gas?) And later when
I wrote the note, "What's a body need?" the poem
Answered, _Rhythm,_ as in, _And on the seventh day
He rested. . ._ full of himself—all that creation—

And hungered for his not-self. In the dream
Of a shattered form
                    within the shattering, the form.
          What shore is this, soul-maker?
And the poem answered, _Leo._

GOD SAW JACOB'S LADDER

Genesis 28:10

God saw Jacob's ladder as a way
        back down and into the rock
from which He'd been released.

Babel could have been that way
        but words had yet to be broken
and here was this kid, delicious,

wishing his way to Him. Finally.
        A dreaming kid. Behold,
he thought, my ticket home!

And so while the angels ballyhooed
        and Jacob fretted
about his seed, down He climbed

in plain sight and what with all
        the hoopla, Jacob
never noticed God step down

and through his mind, into the ground
        of his sleeping self. Felt
only a tug from the wake of Him.

THE WHEELED BLADE

                              Gellman showed me how
to shovel out the pizza pie, slice it into pieces
with the rolling flashing blade. Day one, summer job—
at *Piece O' Pizza*, the original, on Beverly near Fairfax,
in L.A., a first-generation neon *HAD A PIECE LATELY?*
sign blinking above the door.

Gellman of the quick criss-crossing slashing moves.
The controlled and moral beauty of his rage.
He'd slugged me once. When we were kids.
(Our families lived on a bungalow court,
and wrestling over half a Danish I'd lashed out,
off balance, no science at all and missed my punch,
when up came the uppercut, square to my guilty—
                              it *was* his, the Danish—chin.)
His family moved, we lost touch and here we were
the late shift: LAWRENCE, said his Piece O' Pizza badge.
He was on the Jr. Mgr. track.

Larry! I said, pounding out the dough, *Remember Judy?*

Judy Sharfman. Also on the court. Her father
ran the Hebrew School. Crazy Judy, she'd let us
look. *Nymph,* we called her, though really all we did
was look. She'd open her legs—on her back
on the grass—then snap them shut. Jaw-dropped, I
watched in wonder: it was true—as had been told—
                              she didn't have one.
Open-shut-open-shut, Larry said, *I've seen that,*
and chopped the air karate style timed to pass between
the flap-flopping legs. Judy never flinched,
then snapping her knees in a scissors squeeze
completely mashed the hand. (In memory, he wears a cast—)

Remember Judy?

Hell yes! Sharfman. She was fierce. He spun his dough
up through the air. *She wrote my bar mitzvah speech.*

What? I didn't know that.
Though I must have heard him *say* the speech.
Did she write mine? I'd thought it was her father had.
And then and there my words, all words, turned strange
in me. Other. Holy almost: word stream from the cunt spring.
And fearsome, secret: Torah within the Torah flowing
                                through the father book.

(Was I on, unknown to me, the Jr. Poetry track?)

We sloppered on tomato sauce. He showed me how
to crater the crust to make the bubbling lakes of cheese.
Kings of the night shift, we lifted our voices and sang
to the jukebox R & B—*yes it's me 'n I'm in love again!*

And just as I was getting the mind and body hang of it—
the spinning, the ovens, the whirling blade—
clank, one Sunday night went the lock,
lights out, Gellman in his Chevy's yellin', *Seeya!*
Piece O' Pizza's shut, and it was time, September, time,
                                that other wheeled blade, to go.

BAR MITZVAH CHOKE REVISITED

He tried to chant the chant, but caught on something in his throat,
the melody would not come out. You hear it on the tape: there's me,
the prize trained seal, barking Hebrew from the Book—how Jacob
fought a stranger in the middle of the night—and him. Or silence
where he should have been.

He could have read the lousy blessing, there were cheat sheets the
Temple made. But no, he had to sing. His brother, Ted, the oily one,
did _his_ like Eddie Cantor. So how come for my pa, the good, God
couldn't get it to come out? He starts out rough, _Barchu,_ he croaks,
then chokes, like something's in his throat.

Needs me, I wonder if I thought. Or did another thought think me:
How dare you, if he can't sing—and never stop from thinking me—
Let the song of sons go dead—until I sat with him at Cedars. And then
it was too late to sing—_see, sons, what things you are?_ Of that I sing,
too late to sing, how even Jacob had to fight with a stranger in the
night.

AND MIND BEGINS ITS AWESOME BROOD

—_for Annie_

All our dignity consists, then, in thought.
—Pascall

"I don't believe in hell at all—"

      she's 6 1/2 and here we go, iambic
      all the way, doubling the double L
      in a kind of ululation over the dinner plate—

"and I don't _think_ I believe in heaven—"

the step back from certainty nicely caught
by breaking the beat, the thunk midway of think
on the brain: it's one thing to pull the plug on hell

"—but when you die do you just _lie_ there forever? —"

      she wonders through the rhyme
      (Hey, Mr. Death, or, better, Hi!)
      into—smack—the question mark.

"That's boring. Bury me next to Bubba with a pack of cards . . ."

                      'til, clink,

"Sorry, Annie, to tell you this—"

      voice of the brother, 9, the wise,

"but all you do is turn to dirt;
all you'll be forever is dirt;
what you're made of _now_ is dirt . . . "

      and she, interrupted, all fury and spit,
      nailing the meter again, hurls back,

"Fuck you, Jacob, I AM _NOT_ DIRT."

THE TEACHINGS

1. His Garden

I bring him home, sit him down on the back porch
and point to the garden, saying, *Tell me what you see.*
His Garden I write at the top of the page
and think, *Easy. This is going to write itself.*

But, *Street,* is what he says, *a narrow, cobbled street*
& a horse pulling a wagon. Old guy, tattered coat, has got the reins.
Two kids. Legs hanging out the back of the wagon.

I look. One of the kids is me.

2. In Cahoots

I'm under the table and won't come out. My father
is saying to the rabbi, *He says he's a rooster and won't come out.*
It was true, I was a rooster. So the rabbi
gets down on the floor with me, and whispers, *Me, too.*
                              Don't tell, and as you go
                    around being what is called a self,
          don't forget, we're roosters.

3. The Moral Clarity of Compost

He'd start a story saying, *Never, as a rule,*
                              tell anybody anything.
But this is too delicious and delicious overrules.

He was going to teach me how to die but ran out of life to do it in.

Schmuck, he said, *that's the teaching.*

GAZELLE IN THE BERLIN ZOO, 1966

I return to the gazelle, press up against the bars
and she comes to me.
My hand slips through, strokes the curving horn,
bony socket of the eye.
As long as I murmur into her ear,
she will stay as close as the fence allows.

Upon arrival in Berlin, address from an agency in hand,
I knocked at an apartment door, showed the paper
to somebody's grandmother who nodded and asked,
"Sprechen Sie Deutsch?"
I shook my head. "Do you speak English?"
"Nein." A silent moment passed.
She shrugged, drew me in to apples and cloves.

I toured the city, returning each evening to the zoo.
Last night, in Frau Schneider's warm rooms,
we shared spice cookies and tea,
the surprise of broken language.
Later, in the back of a wardrobe,
I found a woolen SS uniform
belonging to her dead husband.

I saw the barbed-wire enclosure, curdled snow,
a woman dripping rags,
the urine-yellow star.

In her dirt compound, the gazelle is fed and sheltered,
but she was meant to fly across the grasslands with a great herd,
outrunning the cheetah
for as long as she could.

She chews on my hair; I hear a muffled sound.
I wonder what she knows about forgiveness.

OLIVE OIL

—for my Sephardic grandmother, Julia Del Bourgo

I remember eyes like sapphires,
dark moles in the folds of her neck,
her bosom skillfully imprisoned in linen.

Olive oil must be deep green and pungent
to evoke other memories,
sautéed fava beans, roasted chicken,
rice blushing with tomato and raisins plump with steam.
Cream puffs for dessert,
flour caught in her diamond ring.

We were fed advice:
> *Never buy a used book; people are dirty.*
> *Those crab apples are sour;*
> *your mouth will pucker up and stay that way, forever;*
> *no one will want you.*
> *We don't take the bus; we'll never have to, God willing,*
> *we take cabs.*
> *Kosher meat is always best; don't try to fool me with that traife*
> *from Albertson's.*

In her birthplace, Massua, Eritrea,
where she could hear lions cry outside the compound walls,
she attended the only school for girls; nuns taught women's work.
On Shabbos, her father, a colonel in the Italian army,
brought in hungry Jews to feed.
Her mother emptied the larder, silently served them.

Before Grandmother's blood broke,
the betrothal was sealed by mail;
the family with its too many girls lacked dowry
and who but a cousin would have her?
Wrapped like a gift against the ocean's cold,
she was shipped to Shanghai,
handwritten recipes in her trunk.
Among the rickshaws on the dock,
a stranger, my grandfather, elegant and contained, in a downpour.

**

After twenty years and two boys,
before Mao marched and the Last Emperor fell,
Grandfather got the family and its fortune out,
settled into the house on Tiger Tail Road in Brentwood,
comfortable among the wealthy and the famous.

She ruled her house with a wave of her hand
and commands in Ladino. She knitted and sewed,
taught the proper way to behave.
> *Don't be familiar with the maid;*
> *she's robbing us blind.*
> *It's not ladylike to run.*
> *Don't wear that frou-frou blouse;*
> *dress well and you, too, will marry a Del Bourgo.*
> *Keep the line pure.*

In her curio cabinet, animals of yellowed ivory, amber and jade:
a small herd of horses, three monkeys, a Pekinese.
Dressed up in dotted swiss,
I was allowed to play with them, but carefully,
behind the striped silk couch with dragon's feet.
> *When I go, all these will be yours.*

But, after Grandfather died,
the antiques buyer with the mustache arrived.
Month by month, the creatures were sold
as I secretly wept in one room, Grandmother in another.

I wear her earrings of platinum and pearls,
make filling for *bourekas* the old way:
stir spinach and onions, ground meat and garlic in sizzling olive oil.
A knob of hard candy between my teeth,
I sip bitter tea from her gold-rimmed cup,
close my eyes, lean against the kitchen counter,
listen for the sound
of the lions' cry.

THE QUEEN OF SHEBA HOTEL, EILAT, ISRAEL, 1966

Leia emerges from the ocean, slick and dripping.
Slips on a white cotton shift,
sandy feet into flip-flops,
climbs exterior stairs to his floor.

Inside his suite,
she leans back against the window frame,
untwines her midnight braids,
combs dreamy furrows.
The sun drapes her neck like a boa,
her fingers fan out over naked breasts
as the foreign man watches,
lounging on a loveseat,
sucking on a cigarette so slowly
the tip barely glows.
Smoke brocades the air.
The man is inert;
only his right hand moves the cigarette
in and out of his mouth.

Like the first time,
he does not touch her,
thrusts American dollars into her crocheted bag—
more than she earns in a month
on her family's kibbutz.

She runs past the village on the beach
where she's visiting with the gypsies,
sheds her clothing,
throws herself into the swells,
through small breakers.

When her purse is heavy
she will sail away from him,
from all of them,
away from Eilat at the arrow point
of this ancient sea.
She floats on her back,
arms spread,
water sloshing melodies in her ears.

A vee of geese
unzips the sky.

ON SPENDING JUST ONE NIGHT
WITH A VERY YOUNG RABBINICAL STUDENT

Night rain the color of shale.
I suggest something and he says,
Do people really do that? And I say,
They do. Come along, if you dare.

And he comes along,
but not too fast.

Fire in the bedroom.
Once, we break for wine and chocolate,
Merlot stain on the pillowcase.
Later, sheets in a turmoil, he says,
I could do this all night
and I say, *You're 18 and yes you can.*

Morning light.
Tender arrangement of limbs on bed
where, briefly, we are bound.
He says, *Maybe one more time,*
then I've got to get back to school,
and I am underneath this landscape of muscle,
his skin smelling like fresh-baked bread.

Later, emerging from the bath,
he mentions the Hebrew word *chet,*
meaning not "sin" but rather "missing the mark,"
the archer having made a mistake
through lack of experience or skill.
I smile, towel him dry.

After breakfast,
he leaves my house,
crunches away on the gravel path.
Underneath the yarmulke,
new strands of sunshine
woven into his hair.

GRANDFATHER'S FUNERAL,
ORTHODOX SEPHARDIC SYNAGOGUE,
LOS ANGELES

We are separated in the foyer.
Father and my younger brother
invited into the great hall with the other men,
while Grandmother and I are barred entry.
Instead, we are ushered up interior stairs
to a gallery where women
and other teen-aged girls
are concealed
behind a wooden screen.

We may not pray aloud or sing.
We peer through leaf-pattern scrollwork,
our faces and bodies properly forgotten,
as men raise their voices in praise of my grandfather
who would drop a dollop of butter
into my soft-boiled eggs,
recite poems he'd written
and ask me questions each week
about how I was doing
in school.

The balcony is stuffy. It is hard to breathe.
The songs and prayers drone in my ears. Hebrew
by others for others.
Grandfather never told me that a woman's role
was to be invisible,
our life's work, silence.

I long to fly down to the temple floor,
a raven with sharpened beak,
patrol back and forth
across the top of his coffin,
flinty eyes toward heaven,
railing against
the thief.

SIKA DEER

In a cemetery in Kobe, Japan,
among the upright stones
with characters like houses under a lowering sky,
lie the graves of my grandfather's people,
Sephardic Jews born on the run.

They had used bamboo for walls against
the salt breath of winter, against
the music of the shamisen, three strings—
one for betrayal
by a business partner,
the second to mourn an infant
lost in this faraway land,
the last for the long letter from Turkey:
since the capstone had been removed,
the archway to the family compound
was collapsing.

Sika deer browse
beside my ancestors.
Red maples reach up,
branches split against the gibbous moon.

Hoof prints in snow-light.

THE LAST JEW OF OSWIECIM

Heavy with tenderness
he prays to God.
Traces the curved space
between her breasts,
before the end of their world—
all torn away.
Flowers of hell, colorless things.

> *the dead see*
> *with hollow eyes*

On the way to a slaughterhouse
others stare through bars
to see beyond breaking shadows.
Death spills over and over—
little box of hours,
bellies full of nails
hands full of stars.

> *the dead talk on*
> *race against time*

He hides through it all and after
lives in a dirt cellar, whispers . . .
come closer wing of rain,
hummingbird of love.
I want your mouth,
your body
your pale seeds of light.

> *Kaddish, syllable by syllable*
> *in the mouth of strangers*

SUNDAY SCHOOL

Sometimes we sat before the Ark
in the sanctuary among velvet
cushions and polished pews.
I crayoned Moses purple,
acted Esther in a Purim play,
and was sure God knew my name.

After class Mother took me
to the seawall.
Sand stretched to the Bay.
We found shells, rocks, glass
worn smooth.
I decide which

to carry home.
Put away, somewhere,
relics of another world
from those days
when I was sure God
knew my name.

REVEILLE

It's funny what can happen
at funerals—at my uncle's,
a man I knew as a child,
then rarely saw,
I remember
how he taught me to jitterbug.
His sons told stories,
the rabbi led kaddish—

I hear a jukebox play,
the Andrews Sisters singing,
"He plays reveille,
the boogie-woogie bugle boy
of Company C."
My uncle, not old or bent,
pulls me off the soda fountain stool,
says, "Niece let's dance,"

and twirls me
out, away,
then close again.
We hold hands,
rock back and forth.
He shows me the steps,
spins me around,
around,
swings my body
across his hips
one, then the other.
Our feet fly
and faces flush,
curly hair
damp with sweat—

sweet laughter that day,
my uncle teaches me to dance.

DEAR YOUNG MAN,

July 10, 1963—

I lean out the window to you. We are
laughing, talking, those minutes before
the train leaves. You kiss my hand,
like something from an old movie. I love

this gesture, and in the moment, you.
Today, reading Polish poets, I remember
arriving that warm sunny day, you, Warsaw—
the ruins, the rebuilding, glimpses of grandeur.

I have Grandfather's address, but his street is
gone. We go to the ghetto, nothing is left:
there are new apartments, and embedded in
concrete, a small plaque. For your family,

three cramped rooms. How frail your father
seems. He speaks softly, while we drink tea.
Your mother serves cake and no one smiles.
We ride your motorbike, follow a narrow

road into the green countryside. There are
cows, tinkling bells, the sweet smell of grass.
I picture the Wizard of Oz. We arrive at
a summer palace, but it's Fidel Castro and

entourage strolling in the gardens. Dear
young man, do you remember that naïve
self-absorbed American girl? I ask for
your forgiveness, and hope you are well.

BECKY

No one rocks me anymore /
no one sings to me the way you did

what would you think if you saw us
what would you think /
women forsaking the Sabbath going
into evening to light who knows where /
What would you think of us /
wearing trousers in synagogue
holding a man's hand while we pray /
oh, Becky would you think it blasphemy /
writing poems with _god_ / spelled on the page
gay avec, you might say, go away
until we slow it down / chant the _shabbos_ prayer
swaying over candles / and Becky / ay ay ay /
your great-great-granddaughters spill it all /
hold nothing back / would you think
that the world you left behind /
would you think it spins out of control?

I can hear you sighing / feel you /
rocking other babies to sleep

VISITING TEREZIN

September 11, 2001,
in this ghetto museum
conversation seeps through closed windows
from the world outside.
At first I think it's on the tape playing inside
of children's voices—ghosts.
Our elderly Jewish guide tells me
I remind her of a cousin who lived in Austria.

Really, it's uncanny she says.
Ghosts: at the cemetery and crematorium,
where we walk among ovens, long cold,
still caked with ash.
Our guide says most Americans don't understand
what war does, we're just too removed.
At home it rains white ash and dust
onto the streets of New York,
onto all of us.

DOCTOR ALEX STONE

I would do my life all over again, no regrets!
Just a lucky son of a bitch
until I slid into eighty, then bam,
slid right out the door.
No painful protocols for me,
I wanted quality of life and some fun
saying my good-byes.
Dear friends told me jokes,
I answered their questions and asked mine,
so much to learn about everyone
I loved in six short months—
held on to Barb, held on tight.
It was cold and wet graveside,
that useless body in the coffin
is no longer me.
I lingered with family while the rabbi said prayers.
When it was over, an old joke came to me.
Jewish man to his friend:
if I live I'll see you Tuesday,
if I die I'll see you Wednesday . . .

SKYLIGHT

Make an opening for daylight in the ark.
Genesis 6:16

There is a torn place in my sky
a hole in the roof of my house
an opening in the crown of my head
where light comes in
and rain
and darkness descends to cover me
but not for so very long
not for all time
not so far forever.
I close my eyes to hide my disbelief
to show no disrespect
and when the open spot becomes a pain I wear a *kipa*
like the hand of God on my head.
Then I can look: and then I can ask:
is the world my shelter
is the world a home
has creation come to an end—
I pray standing up
I'm not ashamed to shout a little
I don't mind if I tremble—
You set me down in one place
and said *talk and talk go ahead name the animals if you want*
but don't talk too much
You said *multiply* and started in with dividing
You said *go add up* and then began to subtract
You spread your *tallit* across the heavens
You set your bow in the clouds and said *Never again*
You left a torn place in the sky
You left a hole in the roof of my house
You left an opening in the crown of my head.

Noach, Genesis 6:9–11:32

MILK AND HONEY

from "Book of Numbers: A War Diary (2003)"

O dear God: the land You have promised us
already has people living in it; and why
didn't we hear that part before the exodus?
So this is the choice, to live as slaves or die
as slaves to war. Now think: some other place
You haven't got? We sent out men to spy
for us, a sorry lot who claim a race
of giants lives up there, but what a lie—
most likely long-lost relatives. Hebron's
a town as old as Esau, walled with stones
they'll gladly throw at us, blood brothers or not.
Couldn't we come in peace, share what we've got
including You, settle down and call
it off? But *No,* You answer. *You must dispossess them all.*

Shelach-lecha, Numbers 13:1–15:41

PRACTICE

Every seventh year you shall practice remission of debts.
Deuteronomy 15:1

How simple it ought to be, to practice compassion
on someone gone, even love him, long as he's not
right there in front of me, for I turned to address him,
as I do, and saw that no one's lived in that spot
for quite some time. O turner-away of prayer—
not much of a God, but he was never meant to be.
For the seventh time I light him a candle; an entire
evening and morning it burns; not a light to see
by, more a reminder of light, a remainder, in a glass
with a prayer on the label and a bar code from the store.
How can he go on? He can't. Then let him pass
away; he gave what light he could. What more
will I claim, what debt of grace he doesn't owe?
If I forgive him, he is free to go.

Re'eh, Deuteronomy 11:16–16:17

BLESSING HIM

In the old stories we tell each other
to keep awake or help us sleep or mark
the way by car to second grade
and back, there is a hero, and there is a test.
Riddles are posed to him, mad questions asked,
mazes of multiple choice; there is a wilderness
to cross, a fast river, a sealed-up
house with a disguised way in
and a spring to the lock; there is a spell:
He doesn't know at first
which power is going to help, intelligence,
force, cunning, so he carries all three,
in amounts that shift shape
as he carries them, as he himself
can change along the way, has trouble sticking
to the story, the assignment, because all stories
are connected and he slides, seeing
he can enter another element, change
the subject, become a creature of water or air,
and then we've all but lost him,
and then what spell is going to call him back?

In the old stories, impostor parents
set the hero to tasks, stealing his time
from dreaming, can't see what kind
of creature he is, can't comprehend his nature,
a contemplative angel in white
wearing red lipstick, doing his nails black. . . . No.
He is sitting at the kitchen table gripping
his pencil with a fist while I put away
the shopping, has to write
a story for school with a set of seven words
starting with *s* and feels the separation
between mind and hand, a trickster spirit
that won't let him do what he knows how;
says in tears because I have gotten mad
that he's no good at thinking of stories, no good at thinking,
but here on the table beside him is a *perfect
report from the teacher*, penciled in his own hand.

In the old stories, for all the while the hero
is being tested, measured, evaluated,
written up, the unforeseen
right answer overthrows the one
only thought right. There is a way out.
In the old stories there are proper words to say:
We are sitting at the kitchen table
blessing him for Shabbat, placing the hands
of fathers on his head and whispering
into his ear the words of burden,
hope, and vow: _Y'sem-cha Elohim_
k'Efrayim v'chi Menashe; may God make you
like the sons of Joseph,
and be gracious to you, and give you peace.
He stills his constant motion;
he lets the hands rest on his head; he likes it;
we don't know ourselves
what power the words have in this story;
do we want him to be what we want
if he has no way of knowing how? The candlelight
as he stares into it lets him enter a little
dream. He is only half tempted to blow it out—

Vayechi, Genesis 47:28–50:26

THE VOICE IN THE FIRE

Preparing to pray is in itself a prayer.
Or so I say. I will begin tomorrow.
Having fled here, though none pursue. Fled where.
Within, far, to the desert place, the sorrow
place. For what I have done. For surely the matter is known.
But see, turn aside, look, the thorn tree, the heart
is not consumed; burning, it does not burn
to ash. It has a voice: Friend, pilgrim, start
now on your way. You can't save your prayer for the world
to come, vagrant one, it is your call, the knowing
to turn and answer, *Wilderness of God,*
hard mountain, I am here. A pilgrim going
to the farthest place is praying, or too can pray
if the place be near, since going is the way.

Shemot, Exodus 1:1–6:1

THE WEIGHT

You must prepare to carry nothing
where you walk,

a God who cannot be seen,
a name you cannot speak—

therefore gather
the most precious of what you have,

and build me something heavy you can carry,
heavy as you want.

I will be weightless in it,

an idea, a promise,
among you, within you—

I will be unbearable. You can bear it.

Over and over you will pick it up
and set it down,

and as you wander
you will lose what you brought forth,

the ark will collapse in your hands,
the stones of the law will break.

Then you will carry me in your minds,
in your mouths—

unbearable as you want. You can bear it.

Terumah, Exodus 25:1–27:19

POTATO MENORAHS

She wanted the children to know how it was to be
poor, to live where it wasn't safe to be a Jew.

*She feels continents of ice below, huge tectonic
plates with stress lines radiating in all directions.*

Each of the eight took an Idaho potato, gouged
nine holes to make a primitive menorah.

*She is seeing dust and stars as galaxies collide,
the millions of years it takes for them to cross.*

They rolled tiny candles of beeswax, gathered at
the low table and lit them together.

*She is considering the possibility that laws of
nature might be shuffled or redefined.*

Together, they said the blessing, but then heat
and candlelight dazzled them into silence.

*She is trying to see a place where edges of matter
dissolve and all things, all people are commingled.*

When the candles blinked out, the eight peeled
the potatoes. Their latkes were out of this world.

HOLOCAUST MUSEUM: CREMATORIUM II

A scale model sculpted from plaster: that's all it is. So why does it have such power? Hundreds of tiny figures walk, move, lie within a pristine world, ice-white like timeless friezes from the pediment of the Parthenon.

Undressing: hats coats gloves scarves dresses jackets shirts shoes stockings panties watches rings lockets	white-faced with shame, they cry white tears remove layers of chalky clothes cover themselves with thin white towels and hands avert white, frightened eyes
Gassing: lock the door bar it check through peepholes Zyklon B: prussic acid pellets drop kill some gone in an instant all in 20 minutes then pump in fresh air	here they howl their silent white screams clutch the albino bodies of their children stare in dull-white horror at showerheads step on whited bodies of the fallen swim through a tide of white death and with colorless lips rimming black-holes struggle toward the white brink of Lethe
Cremation: shave womens' heads pull gold teeth check body orifices for hidden valuables nothing human left 3 or 4 to an oven depending on size only 1,000 a day a waste when they could gas 7 times that	white stretchers carried by white guards white cordwood-stiff bodies to be pillaged white-faced, white-shouldered Jews shove whitened bodies of the dead into white ovens while grim white-starched guards oversee white world still and bloodless where white men sought whiteness and now we need white to purge evil just white all white white nothingness only white white white white white white white white white white . . .

WINTER SOLSTICE

1. Baba

In the cellar, on a rusted lawn chair by the furnace,
I find our Baba. Wearing black lace-ups,
a dress with hand-sewn buttonholes—identical
except where her waist makes one grin, she stares
until hectic spots stain her cheeks. Light stipples
fly-specked windows, sheens hairnet spider-webbing
her forehead below folds of *sheitel*. Around her:

detritus of decades. Our cellar is for useless things.
First, we stockpile them by the stairs. Then they
molder on shelves or atop the child-sized workbench:
flowerpots, Lincoln Logs, last year's checks.
Eyes passing over all, aware of heat and drip, I
ask our Baba, *What are you doing down here?*

Rolling socks, she says. *Like most* bubbes *I stay home
and roll socks.* Now her cheeks deepen. *Or sometimes,
at night, I roll in sweet-scented hay . . .*

        Baba, it's dark and damp, I tell her. *You don't
belong down here.* She layers one thick-fingered hand
over the other. *But I do, my Dumpling,* she says, *because
upstairs in your fine house, I forget to roll and can't
even remember my name.*

2. Mother

Poised at her scale, Mother—keeper of family myths—
weighs truth against fabrication. _It never happened,_
she insists. Baba was Grampa Jack's mother's mother,
dead before you were born.

> _Still,_ I insist, _she was there, sitting in_
the dark, dressed in worsted, with hands like mine
and a long face. And she spoke to me._

Mother, unwilling to pardon unreality, recalibrates,
scoffs at me. _Then it's her photograph you remember._
We stored it in the cellar between our furnace
and the hot water heater.

3. Self

Shuffle, step, shuffle, step. In the cellar I am tapping
all the bright things Mother and others tell me
are not true. _Shuffle, scuff, turn._ Look. Then look again.
My cane, my hat—both are props, for I am not yet Baba,
not yet my mother. Still, upstairs, I can't practice on
satin-finish floors because I'll scar them. So, using
the workbench as barre, I dance—days are short now—
against time, against rage.

> Baba danced in Szumsk, I'm sure,
but never here. Looking on, she finds me disconcerting as
my house: strong-hipped, grown woman in skivvies,
socks, and TeleTones tapping into gathering darkness.
Why? she asks. _Because,_ I answer, eyeing squared hands.
Shuffle, flap. Shuffle-hop, toe. Because as winter comes,
I, too, need time—_shuffle, roll_—to contemplate
sweet-scented hay.

CEMETERIES: ALL OR NOTHING

For it is all or nothing in this life, for there is no other.
—Larry Levis

Fresh snow   long johns   scarves
Flat tombstones   gloved fingers stiff
Boot-scrape the snow   Solomon Levi 1877
Our great-great-great-grandfather   Then
Matilda his wife   uncovered
Elation   *The small bones & X's on stones*

Another cemetery   Charlotte the suicide
Unmentioned   almost gone
The next swipe   Father   Hello Dad
How did we get so old   as old as you
Crazy to be here at six degrees   Not yet
Smart enough to come out of the cold

Graveyard truths   Our mixed marriages
German Jews and across the road the Poles
Isaac and Rose   The road   Saw *Our Town*
Two months ago   The dead impassive
Seeing us seeing them   asking
Why we come on this road   why we care

One day   go back to one ordinary day
Our father with us   years ago at the lake
Saying   cup your fingers when you stroke
Open your eyes   Swimming's not sleeping
Don't breathe too often or roll   Be a knife
In water   Sharper   lighter than air

Snow muffles   mystifies   Brush the snow
Reveal a name   Each a new sleeper
Uncovered   Great-Great-Grandfather lying
Between his sister-wives   the first
Unnamed infant with her   lost at birth
I'm not coming   Mother had said   I'll be

There soon enough   but not near Uncle Mel
And toss out that vase of fake roses
A puzzle   Who left those gaudy yellow
Heads for snow to turn to cotton bolls
In the pristine whiteness   no small stones
Jews leave them to remember   We make

Small snowballs instead   Glee and im-
Permanence   Here mortality should weigh us
Down yet doesn't   For today   we're immortals
In the silence of snow   only boot-creak
And the bell-tones of our old girl-voices
For now we're safe   We think summer cotton

And sun   time at the lake   and still like
"Graveyard in Snow"   Friedrich's burned
Canvas   we will imprint this
Preserve its pale scene   everyone here
Even Thyra   dead at twelve   as Mother
her namesake   creeps toward a hundred

Slowly we tromp past Alsace and Szumsk
And sheen of their white blankets
We tuck in the old ones   hold each
Other   Sleep well   we say   yet don't ask us
To join you   We'll be at the lake   scattered
In high summer   Laugh with us then

Our uncupped fingers   our rolling and roiling
Eyes no longer open   breath no longer held
Wind-crimped water   a faux-field of snow
Bodies unknifed   light in late sun
There   rocks everywhere   Our children
Will skip them for Matilda and Solomon

For Isaac   Rose   Charlotte   Abe   Thyra
Father and soon   Mother   *Sweet Nothing*
Sweet sweet Nothing   For the last
Nothing   White and without prints   For us no
Graveyards   Instead moving water and skipped
Stones   A ripple of stones to remember all

TO OUR CHILDREN

Instead of using the staircase,
risk the tendriled stalks of ivy
and drop into the muddy copse below.

Your great-grandfathers understood mud
as they slogged from village to village
peddling pots and ribbons and scissors.

They knew days with no light, nights
with no heat, years with no safety—
years of pogroms, famine, and loss.

But, still, you may collar their essence
if, shaking pearls from your ears,
you can know wet boots and windfall.

CONTRIBUTORS' NOTES

DAN BELLM

I came to Judaism by choice in my late twenties; entered the *mikveh* as a convert at the age of thirty-six; and became a bar mitzvah in my jubilee (fiftieth) year. "The voice in the fire" was part of my bar mitzvah sermon on the Torah portion, *Shemot.* My shul is Congregation Sha'ar Zahav in San Francisco, a Reform synagogue founded over three decades ago by gay and lesbian Jews, and I am married to a rabbi. I have been writing poetry in the midrashic tradition for a long time now, in varying spirits of inquiry, doubt, devotion, anguish, bemused disbelief, outrage, love, and surrender, and I have taught writing and midrash to Jews and non-Jews from high school age to eighty.

Biographical Notes

Dan Bellm has published three books of poetry, most recently *Practice: A Book of Midrash* (Sixteen Rivers Press, 2008), winner of a California Book Award and named one of the year's top ten poetry books by the *Virginia Quarterly Review.* He is also a widely published translator of fiction and poetry from Spanish, and an instructor in literary translation for Antioch University, Los Angeles, and for New York University. He lives with his husband and son in San Francisco.

Acknowledgments

All six poems appeared in *Practice: A Book of Midrash* (Sixteen Rivers Press, 2008). "Skylight" was originally published in *Tikkun,* "Blessing Him" in *The Threepenny Review,* "The Weight" in *Boston College Magazine,* "Practice" in Solo, and "Milk and Honey" in *Image.*

ROSE BLACK

I began with the deep split I felt between my mother's strong Jewish roots and my father's strong Catholic ones, with their alienation from their own religions and their own families, with the pain and loss that was always spilling out, in spite of their attempts to hide it. I breathed this in. My father's family disowned him when he left the Church, years before he met my mother. And neither my mother nor her family ever forgot that she had married a gentile. She eloped with my handsome, much older father six weeks after they met, and hid that secret from her parents for more than two years. When they finally heard the news, they said no, it couldn't be true. They were shocked and enraged. So although my mother told me I would always be Jewish, I felt I could never be Jewish enough to *really* be Jewish. While I was growing up in Washington, D.C., our family attended All Souls Unitarian Church, where mixed marriages were accepted. We sang about brotherhood and listened to brilliant, intellectual sermons. But it all felt too watery to me. I yearned for the grounding of ritual and tradition, the stories, that my parents grew up with. I came to believe there was one religion that was the true religion, and it was up to me to find it. I wandered from church to church, synagogue to synagogue, searching for a place to belong, a place where all my fragmented parts could come together. Eventually, I found other people with issues similar to mine. Most importantly, I found poetry and poets. Now I could take whatever I wanted from my parents' past, all the traditions and stories (like my mother's brothers sneaking out to the garage at night to fry bacon) and make them my own. There is nothing watery about a good poem.

Biographical Notes

Rose Black lives by the Union Pacific Railroad tracks in Oakland, California, where she and her husband operate Renaissance Stone, a studio and supply source for stone sculptors. Her poetry has been widely published in literary journals and anthologies, including *RUNES, The South Carolina Review, Wisconsin Review, Ninth Letter, Spillway,* and *Slant.* Her book *Clearing* was published in 2005 and reviewed in the Great American Pin Up in May 2005. A second book, *Winter Light,* was published in 2008. Both *Clearing* and *Winter Light* were accepted by Yale's Beinecke Library for the Yale Collection of American Literature. Black is currently associate editor of the *Marin Poetry Center Anthology.*

Acknowledgments

"Inside," *Carquinez Poetry Review* and *Clearing* (Moorpark Press, 2005); "A History of Poland" and "Bad Sheep," *Winter Light* (Moorpark Press, 2008); "A History of Poland," *Schuylkill Valley Journal of the Arts;* "Torah in the Basement" and "Washing the Body," *Poetica.*

CHANA BLOCH

I grew up between two cultures—my parents' *shtetlekh* in the Ukraine and our little shtetl in the Bronx. My mother lit the candles every Friday evening and my father lit his cigarette from the candles, so naturally I kept asking, Who am I? I came to poetry and translation in my twenties as a means to self-definition. I turned up some valuable clues in the process of translating from Yiddish (poems by Jacob Glatstein and Abraham Sutzkever, stories by Isaac Bashevis Singer) and Hebrew (the biblical Songs of Songs, Israeli poets Yehuda Amichai and Dahlia Ravikovitch). My own poetry has increasingly found its way to the time-honored Jewish practice of arguing with the tradition. At seventy I am still asking; the answers keep changing.

Biographical Notes

Chana Bloch, www.chanabloch.com, is the author of four books of poems, most recently *Mrs. Dumpty* (winner of the Felix Pollak Prize) and *Blood Honey* (winner of the Poetry Society of America's Di Castagnola Award). She is co-translator of six books of poetry from Hebrew, including *The Song of Songs* (now a Modern Library Classic), *The Selected Poetry of Yehuda Amichai* and his *Open Closed Open* (winner of the PEN Prize for Poetry in Translation), and *Hovering at a Low Altitude: The Collected Poetry of Dahlia Ravikovitch*. Bloch is professor emerita and former chair of English and Creative Writing at Mills College.

Acknowledgments

"Flour and Ash," "Potato Eaters," "The New World," "Brothers," "The Messiah of Harvard Square," and "The Dark of Day," *Blood Honey* (Autumn House Press, 2009). Winner of the Alice Fay Di Castagnola Award of the Poetry Society of America, selected by Jane Hirshfield. "The Converts," *The Secrets of the Tribe* (Sheep Meadow Press, 1981). Finalist in the Yale Younger Poets Award. "The Messiah of Harvard Square," *Poetry* and *Pushcart Prize XXIX*. "Brothers," *Kenyon Review*. "The Dark of Day" and "The New World," *Michigan Quarterly Review*, reprinted in *Jewish in America*, editors. Sara Blair and Jonathan Freedman (University of Michigan Press, 2004) and *When She Named Fire,* editor Andrea Hollander Budy (Autumn House Press, 2009). "Potato Eaters," *The Reform Jewish Quarterly.* " Flour and Ash," *Field.* ("Flour and Ash" is dedicated to Gale Antokal, the Berkeley artist whose words and drawings inspired the poem.)

RAFAELLA DEL BOURGO

I came out of the egg an atheist and nothing in my upbringing or environment ever changed my mind about that, but I always felt 100% Jewish. Mother was Ashkenazi, Father Sephardic. Unfortunately, my family members were uninterested in passing along stories about their lives. My mother's family immigrated to Canada during the Russian pogroms. They all spoke Yiddish. My maternal grandparents never mentioned their childhoods at all. Maybe their lives in the Old Country were too fraught with misery to rehash, their time in Canada too boring to mention. My father's mother and father were both Del Bourgos, second cousins. His part of the family lived in Turkey until it became too uncomfortable. On the way to Japan, my grandfather was born in New York City and thus was an American. He and others of his extended family lived in Kobe, Japan. My grandmother's part of the family was from Italy but her father was a colonel in the Italian army stationed in Massaua, Eritrea, a port city on the Red Sea. As a child, she was betrothed to my grandfather, and when she turned eighteen, she was sent by ship from Africa to Shanghai, where they were married. My father was born and raised in Shanghai. In the early days of Mao, my grandfather, sensing a coming storm, brought his family to California. My grandfather never spoke to me of his life. My grandmother mentioned a few things about her time in Africa and told me one story about China. Their native tongue was Ladino. We did eat "regular Jewish food" at home but my grandmother's cooking was more exotic, and most delicious. Sunday nights she'd make borekas (small enclosed pies of meat, cheese and/or spinach) for us to take to school for lunches. Recently, during a bout of the stomach flu, I sent my husband to Saul's for Jewish penicillin— chicken soup with matzoh balls. I know that there is a serious religious component to the lives and identities of many Jews. My Jewishness is secular but nonetheless authentic, and I am filled to the brim with it.

Biographical Notes

Rafaella Del Bourgo's writing has appeared in journals such as *Caveat Lector, Puerto Del Sol, Rattle,* and *The Bitter Oleander.* She has won many awards, including the Lullwater Prize for Poetry in 2003 and, in 2006, the Helen Pappas Prize in Poetry and the New River Poets Award. In 2007 and 2008, she won first place in the Maggi Meyer Poetry Competition. The League of Minnesota Poets awarded her first place in 2009. In 2010, "Olive Oil" won first place for the Alan Ginsberg Poetry Awards. Del Bourgo's first collection of poetry, *I Am Not Kissing You,* was published in 2003. She has traveled the world and lived in Tasmania and Hawaii. She teaches college-level English and lives in Berkeley with her husband and three cats.

Acknowledgments

"Sika Deer," *Oberon Poetry Magazine.* "Gazelle in the Berlin Zoo," *Poppyseed Kalache.* "On Spending Just One Night with a Very Young Rabbinical Student," *Caveat Lector.* "Grandfather's Funeral," Nimrod. "Olive Oil," *Paterson Literary Review.*

MARGARET KAUFMAN

Mostly Jewish, our family has first cousins with a Jewish mother and Methodist father. Visiting the church-sponsored children's program during a summer visit to Arkansas, I was tactfully given the 121st Psalm to memorize for their program. That was the easy part. More difficult was having a child place her hands on my head feeling for horns. The teacher intervened to say that Jews did not have them. When my father, away in the Army (circa 1944), found out, he insisted I no longer attend play school at the church. My Arkansas grandfather was the only physician who would treat the local African-American community. His values were instilled in his children and grandchildren. Early on, it was clear that being Jewish wasn't something to take for granted. Back in St. Louis, our home was informal, but on most Friday nights, we lit candles for the Sabbath. In Arkansas, we lit them, but not often. "Down home," catfish was served regularly, with turnip greens and corn bread. Back home, we had lamb, beef, salads, and corn bread, too. I was probably twelve before I saw a challah. My St. Louis grandparents lived half a block away. My grandma played mah jong, made cabbage rolls, and jams from the fruit trees in their backyard. My parents were active in our Temple life: eventually, my father served as its president. Family traditions on both sides of the family stressed learning to understand others and respecting their views. My own involvement in synagogue life—as president at Sherith Israel, where my three children were bar or bat mitzvahed; in community work; and in teaching writing—has grown from family example, and I try to instill those values in my children. We lit candles on Friday nights, and now they do as well.

Biographical Notes

Born in St. Louis, Missouri, Margaret Kaufman began to write in elementary school, encouraged by a neighbor who was a writer and told Kaufman that someday she would be, too. Decades later, she writes fiction and poetry and has won honors in both genres, including two Jessamyn West awards from the Napa Writers Conference, an Anna Rosenberg award, and most recently, an award from *Nimrod*. Her books include letterpress editions of *Aunt Sallie's Lament, Praise Basted In, Deep in the Territory* (The Janus Press, Vermont), Claire Van Vliet. and *Sarah's Sacrifice* (Gefn Press, London). Under supervision by Van Vliet, Chronicle Books printed a trade edition of *Aunt Sallie's Lament.* Kaufman's most recent publications are *Snake at the Wrist* (2002) and *Inheritance* (2010), both from Sixteen Rivers Press. Kaufman has taught poetry classes for over twenty years; she is a faculty member at the Fromm Institute, University of San Francisco. Kaufman lives in Marin County, California, with her life partner Joseph Bodovitz.

Acknowledgments

"Paint," *Snake at the Wrist* (Sixteen Rivers Press, 2002). "Lot's Wife," *Ploughshares*; republished in *Snake at the Wrist*. "Called," "Two Years Later, Yarzheit," and "The Starting Hour," *Inheritance* (Sixteen Rivers Press, 2010). "Tawny Avatar" and "October," *Nimrod*; republished in *Inheritance*.

JACQUELINE KUDLER

My Jewish identity, like my female identity, has never been a subject that much concerned me: it just *is*. Perhaps growing up in Brooklyn—a completely Jewish universe that stretched for miles in every direction—contributed to this particular assessment of myself and of my place in the world. I tended to view the major players in the Torah—Abraham, Sarah, Isaac, Rebecca, Jacob—much as I did my Brooklyn aunts and uncles: all affable, earnest, slightly shopworn, and all connected to me through our shared bloodline, their stories part of the family history that shaped who I am as a human being and consequently as a poet.

Biographical Notes

Jacqueline Kudler lives in Sausalito, California, and teaches classes in memoir writing and literature at the College of Marin in Kentfield. She serves as an advisory director on the board of Marin Poetry Center and is a founding member of Sixteen Rivers Press. Her poems have appeared in numerous reviews, magazines, and anthologies. Her full-length poetry collection, *Sacred Precinct*, was published by Sixteen Rivers Press in 2003. She was awarded the Marin Arts Council Board Award in 2005 and the Marin Poetry Center Lifetime Achievement Award in 2010.

Acknowledgments

"Lot's Wife," *Sacred Precinct* (Sixteen Rivers Press, 2003). "Glass," *Convolvulus*; " Sarah," *Other Testaments* and *The Marin Poetry Center Anthology*; and "Revelation," *Terminus* were republished in *Sacred Precinct*.

MELANIE MAIER

I grew up in San Francisco. raised by a committee of Jewish relatives—parents, grandparents, aunts, and uncles. My parents met when my mother was in high school and married when she graduated. They divorced when I was two, and until Mother remarried we lived with my maternal grandparents. Theirs was a lively home filled with love, family, Judaism, and the Yiddish theater. My great-grandmother ruled the kitchen. I got to shop with her for Pesach and all the holidays. My paternal grandmother attended synagogue every Saturday morning, and sometimes she took me. However, there were Christmas trees in my mother's and father's houses. As a young child, I believed in God and Santa Claus. Growing up in San Francisco in the forties and fifties, I was part of the non-Jewish world around me. Then and now (married to a child of the Holocaust), I am home in my Jewish one.

Biographical Notes

Melanie Maier lives in Marin County, California. She has published two chapbooks, *The Art of Everyday* and *The Land of Us*, and a poetry book, *sticking to earth*. Her work has appeared and is forthcoming in many publications and anthologies, including *In Posse Review, Drash, The Fourth River, Phoebe, The South Carolina Review,* and *The Southern California Review*. Internationally, her work has appeared in *Gazeta Wyborcza,*Warsaw, Poland.

Acknowledgments

"Becky," *RiverSedge;* "Dear Young Man," *Gazeta Wyborcza,* Warsaw, Poland; " Doctor Alex Stone," *The Southern California Review;* "Last Jew of Oswiecim," *Drash: Northwest Mosaic.* "Reveille," *The Land of Us* (Pudding House Publications, 2008) "Sunday School," and "Visiting Terezin" appeared in *sticking to earth* (Conflux Press, 2008).

MURRAY SILVERSTEIN

Born in 1943, I was raised in the Los Angeles borscht belt along Fairfax Avenue. My father's parents, Eastern European Jews who left early, had zigzagged their way west (New York to Missouri to Ohio to California) with six children during the Great Depression. My mother was a gentile who left her family behind (I never met a one) when she married, and, throughout my childhood, passed herself off as a Jew. I myself didn't know until after my bar mitzvah, so there's a reticent, Midwest Episcopalian voice lurking within my Jewish identity. We were officially Reform Jews, but my father took me to the Orthodox temple—a little neighborhood shul—to light the yahrzeit candles for his parents, and this place (as intended) scared the bejeezus out of me. The mumbled, half-chanted sound of the davening, the mysterious, grief-laden kaddish, the triumphant Shema, the memorial candles blazing in the darkened shop-front—all of that's there, no doubt, the ur-poem in the basement of my brain. The kaddish is the most magical-sounding thing I know, still. As a kid, I was a duty-bound Jew, running on automatic. But years later, in my forties, at the end of an eight-year psychoanalysis, I found my way back to poetry (a repressed adolescent love) via the Tanakh. For a couple of years, I read it like a thriller, couldn't put it down, and wrote a book's worth of midrash on the various stories, characters and predicaments—Genesis, Psalms, Song of Songs, Ezekiel, the whole journey. As an architect, I found myself particularly drawn to the Solomon story, culminating in the First Temple, which I read as the achievement of imaginative space, a kind of reified unconscious. The Tanakh became for me the book that "builds" the temple: the temple within the text that, in its innermost space (where even the priests went only once a year) both contains, and is contained by, the word: In short, poetry!

Biographical Notes

Murray Silverstein's first book of poetry, *Any Old Wolf* (Sixteen Rivers Press, 2006), received the Independent Publisher's bronze medal for poetry. Also for Sixteen Rivers, he produced the poetry CD *Naming the Rivers*, and was executive editor of the anthology *The Place That Inhabits Us: Poems of the San Francisco Bay Watershed*. A practicing architect and coauthor of four books about architecture, including *A Pattern Language* (Oxford University Press, 1977). Silverstein lives in Oakland, California.

Acknowledgments

"And Mind Begins Its Awesome Brood," "God Saw Jacob's Ladder," and "Bar Mitzvah Choke Revisited," *Any Old Wolf* (Sixteen Rivers Press, 2006).

SUSAN TERRIS

When I speak before any Jewish group, I always tell the group I am a product of a mixed marriage, because my mother's family were German Jews and my father's were Polish Jews. (Yes . . . a joke.) Both sides of my family had emigrated to the United States in the 1880s and left their family histories behind. When I asked my father about my great-grandfathers, he always said, "Peddlers and tailors." When I asked about my great-great grandfathers, he said, "In the old country, we were all horse thieves." (Another joke . . . sort of.) But, despite no Yiddish and few handed-down memories of the old country, I grew up in St. Louis as part of a fairly observant Reform Jewish household. My parents went to synagogue on Friday nights and were active in local and national Jewish charities. My father was president of our synagogue, and I was one of those odd children who actually loved Sunday School, where I got to be in drama and in choir. These activities steeped me in words and song until I began to dream of becoming a writer. But, apart from my parents and Sunday School, I've always had a strong sense of Jewish identity, because I felt my last name, Dubinsky, identified me as a Jew wherever I went. In school and in communities where Jews were a minority, I was a dark-haired, dark-eyed Dubinsky. So, early in life, like most writers, I took on the role of outsider.

Biographical Notes

Susan Terris, http://www.susanterris.com, is the author of 5 poetry books including *Contrariwise, Natural Defenses,* and *Fire Is Favorable to the Dreamer.* Her newest book is *The Homelessness of Self* (Arctos Press, 2011). Terris' work has appeared in many publications, including *The Iowa Review, Field, The Journal, The Southern Review, Denver Quarterly,* and *Ploughshares.* A poem from *Field* was published in *Pushcart Prize XXXI.* Terris, the author of 13 chapbooks, had two published in 2009—*The Wonder Bread Years* and *Double-Edged*—and two more in 2010: *Bar None and Chapbook on the Marketing of the Chapbook.* For seven years, with CB Follett, she edited *RUNES: A Review of Poetry.* She is now editor of *Spillway* and a poetry editor for two online publications, *Pedestal Magazine* and *In Posse Review.* She does private editing of manuscripts and teaches workshops on the chapbook. In addition, with CB Follett, she runs weekend workshops taught by U.S.C. professor and poet David St. John. She lives in San Francisco with her husband, David. In her spare time, she is the grandmother of twelve.

Acknowledgments

"Potato Menorahs," *Poetica.* "Holocaust Museum: Crematorium II," *Eye of the Holocaust* (Arctos Press, 1999) and *Fire Is Favorable to the Dreamer* (Arctos Press, 2003). "Winter Solstice," *Curved Space* (La Jolla Poets Press, 1998) and the anthology *Nice Jewish Girl* (Penguin Books, 1996). "Cemeteries: All or Nothing," *Maggid.* "To Our Children," *Jewish Spectator;* republished in *Eye of the Holocaust* (Arctos Press, 1999) and the anthology *Bittersweet Legacy* (University Press of America, 2001). (Epigraph and italicized lines in "Cemeteries: All or Nothing" from "At the Grave of My Guardian Angel: St. Louis Cemetery, New Orleans", by Larry Levis.)

SIM WARKOV

My grandparents came to the United States and Canada from Poland and Russia. The *Zaydeh* (grandfather) was immersed in Torah, Talmud, and prayer. His children, my Uncle Yankel and Uncle Moishe, my Aunt Babtzeh, and my father, Mendel, called him der Tateh (the father). My father visited him virtually every day. Der Tateh's wishes ranked supreme. Eastern European patriarchy ruled. My parents observed kashrut and the major holidays, but not the Sabbath or many of the mitzvoth expected of the Orthodox. I call my parents traditional Jews. Above all, my father valued *Wissen*— knowledge—not piety. His library of Hebrew and Yiddish books (now lodged in the National Library in Ottawa, Canada) was part of my cultural landscape. Through my mother (Rose Greenberg), I claim kinship with Chaim Nachman Bialik, a giant among the first generation of modern Hebrew poets. My boyhood in Winnipeg, Manitoba, left little space for free play and idle curiosity: public schooling from 9 to 4, an intensive Jewish education Monday through Thursday from 5 to 6:30 and Sunday from 11 to 12:30. Shabbat services from 9 to 12 rounded out the week. This regimen started in grade three and endured until grade ten. All in the name of *Wissen*. Today, my Jewish identity is tied to my second language, Hebrew, and to a lesser degree, to Yiddish. Yes, my father prevailed, but the *Zaydeh* did not. I think of myself as a secular Jew.

Biographical Notes

Born in Chicago, raised in Winnipeg, Canada, Sim Warkov moved to the Bay Area from Connecticut in 1997 and took up movement/dance with Anna Halprin. He tried his hand at poetry in 1998 and has been at it ever since. His work appeared in *Parallel Verses* (2007), *Rattle*, and several anthologies, including the *Marin Poetry Center Anthology* and *Cloud View Poets* (Arctos Press). He published his first collection of poems, Reaching, in 2006 and his second volume, *Thin Soils*, in 2009. (Translation of the epigraph from the Hebrew for" News from Andalusia" by Sim Warkov.)

Acknowledgments

"Alphabet," *Thin Soils*, 2009. "Mezuzah on My Mind," *Reaching*, 2006. "Sabbath at Starbucks in Los Gatos," *Rattle*; republished in *Thin Soils*.